This Walker Book belongs to:

_____

_____

_____

For Grace and Rose, who always shine on stage.
– K. H.

To Lucca and Vicente, you're my favourite kind of trouble-makers!
– G. K.

First published 2023 by Walker Books Ltd, 87 Vauxhall Walk, London SE11 5HJ
in association with The Royal National Theatre, London SE1 9PX

2 4 6 8 10 9 7 5 3 1

Text © 2023 Katherine Halligan
Illustrations © 2023 Guilherme Karsten

The right of Katherine Halligan and Guilherme Karsten to be identified as author and illustrator
respectively of this work has been asserted in accordance with the Copyright, Designs and Patents Act 1988

This book has been typeset in Georgia

Printed in China

British Library Cataloguing in Publication Data: a catalogue record
for this book is available from the British Library

ISBN 978-1-4063- 9264-7

www.walker.co.uk

LOLA
SAVES *the*
SHOW

KATHERINE HALLIGAN
Illustrated by **GUILHERME KARSTEN**

WALKER BOOKS
AND SUBSIDIARIES
LONDON • BOSTON • SYDNEY • AUCKLAND

National
Theatre

Shhh!
It's opening night!
The lights go down.
The theatre is dark.
Children whisper
and wriggle.
Someone giggles.
Programmes rustle.
The play is about to begin!

Backstage, Lola is excited for her grand entrance.

Oliver is excited too.

"Lolaaa!" he calls. "Hurry – it's almost your time to shine!"

Lola and Oliver are best friends. They understand each other.

QUICK CHANGE ROOM

"Beginners, please!"
Clipboard Charlie calls.
"Stage left for Lola's cue."

Lola is busy imagining the smell of the flowers thrown
by her adoring audience. It is almost show time!

"First, it's toilet time," says Big Ed.

Big Ed thinks he is in charge of Lola, but Lola
knows *she* is in charge of Big Ed.

**Ewww!** Big Ed is very happy that Lola is not a horse...

"Well done, Lola!" says Oliver. "You're going to be a star."

**"Mehhh!"** says Lola. She cannot wait to shine.

Lola is ready to step on stage when ... **oh no!**
She realizes that something is missing. The Very
Important Handkerchief is not on the prop table!

*AND NO ONE ELSE
HAS NOTICED!*

Lola loves the Very Important Handkerchief because
it is red. Red is her favourite colour.

The Person Who Gives Her Carrots must have the handkerchief. Lola knows that without it, the show will be a disaster!

Lola must find the Very Important Handkerchief!
Lola must save the show!

Lola starts to run away from the stage as fast as she can.

"Lola, wait!" Big Ed and Oliver squeal softly.

"Mehhh!" answers Lola.

GREEN ROOM

Lola skitters into the Place Where People Chat.
But she has no time to talk!

Mmm!

The Very Important Handkerchief
is **NOT** there.

Next, Lola dashes up to the
Stupendous Space of Delicious Dresses,
where she spots a fabulously fetching
red gown. Lola licks her lips...

"LOLA!" shouts Oliver.

In her excitement, Lola almost forgets about the Very Important Handkerchief.

Then Lola remembers. And she's off…

Lola scampers into the Room of Fluffy Stuff
and Powder Puffs.

"LOLA, WAIT!" shrieks the Man with the Spiky Brushes.

"LOLA, NO!" cries the Lady with the Big Wigs.

"She's not being naughty," gasps Oliver.
"She knows something we don't know!"

"Mehhh!" says Lola.

Lola darts through the Hall with Pointy Pokey Things.

The Very Important Handkerchief is not there!

It is not in the Place People Prance ...

... or the Spot
of Silly Sounds ...

... or even the Flash and Bang Box.

It's not in the Cupboard of Tasty Treats.
So many handkerchiefs, but none of them red!

Lola looks around in the Room of Weird and Wonderful Worlds
until she feels another rumble in her tummy...

"*Lola, don't!*" shout Oliver and Big Ed together.

So Lola does not. No time for that sort of business now.
She must save the show!

Nothing can stop Lola! She is a truly excellent climber.
Big Ed is not.

Up Lola climbs, higher and higher.

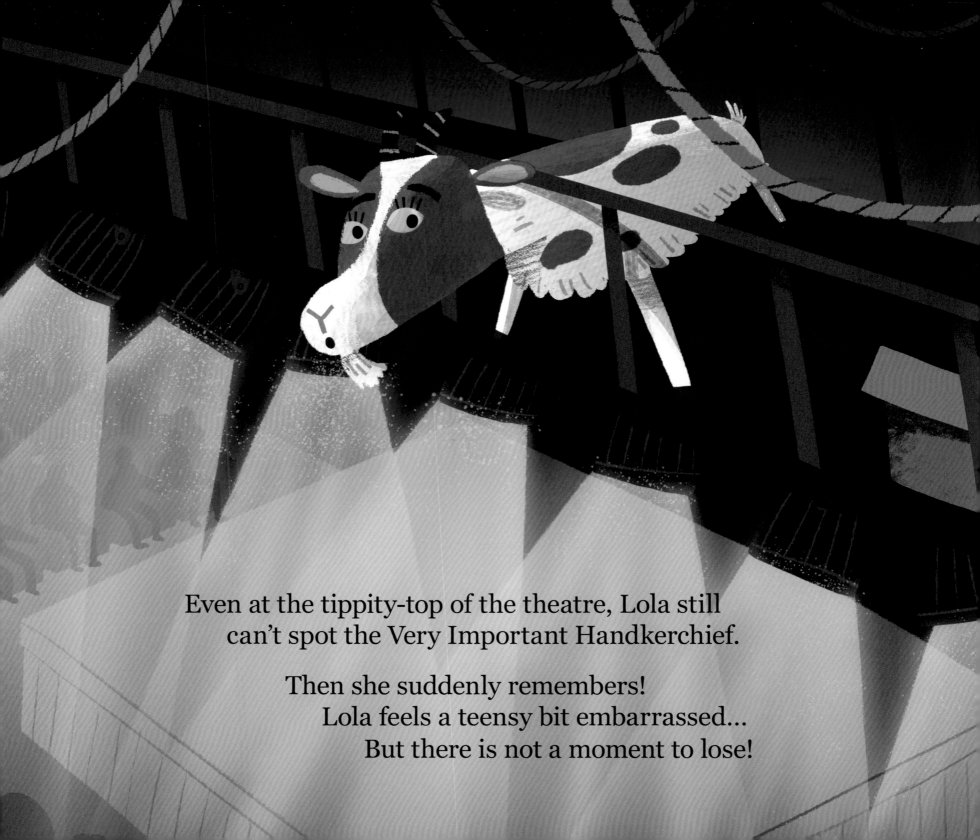

Even at the tippity-top of the theatre, Lola still
can't spot the Very Important Handkerchief.

Then she suddenly remembers!
Lola feels a teensy bit embarrassed...
But there is not a moment to lose!

Lola scrabbles back down, then through the Room of Weird and Wonderful Worlds (*hmmm!*),

the Cupboard of Tasty Treats (*mmm!*),

the Stupendous Space of Delicious Dresses (*ahhh!*),

the Room of Fluffy Stuff and Powder Puffs (terribly tempting!),

and the Place Where People Chat (no time to talk!),

the Flash and Bang Box (*crash!*),

the Spot of Silly Sounds
(*la, la, la!*),

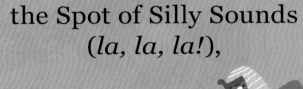

the Hall with Pointy Pokey
Things (*ouch!*),

the Place People Prance
(*tappity tap!*),

until, finally ...

... Lola is back where she started.

And there, in the pile of Lola's Favourite Dressing Up Things, is the Very Important Handkerchief.

"Lola!" sighs Oliver.
"Lola!" gasps Clipboard Charlie.
"Lola!" weeps Big Ed.

But there is no time to waste. The show must go on.

At last, without a
second to spare, the
Person Who Gives Her
Carrots steps onto the stage.

Lola makes her grand entrance.
It is her moment to shine!

And shine she does!
The crowd love Lola and Lola loves the crowd.
If only they knew how she saved the show!

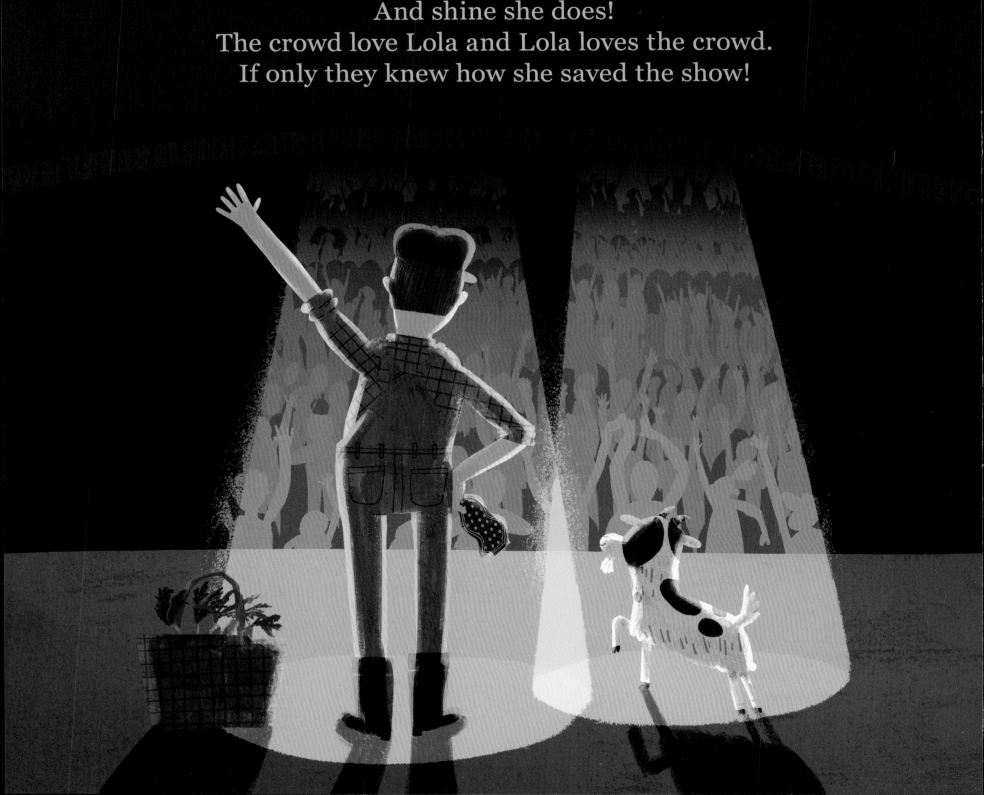

But something is still missing...
No one has thrown any flowers for Lola!
What sort of a theatre is this?

Lola hangs her head in sadness.

"*Lola,*" says Oliver, who always understands her, "you were a real star today."

"***You saved the show!***" everyone shouts, clapping.

Then Oliver gives Lola a wonderful surprise...

Because Oliver loves Lola
and Lola loves Oliver.

BACKSTAGE MAGIC

The theatre is an amazing place. But creating magic takes a lot of hard work! Let's find out more about the people and places Lola discovers on her backstage adventure.

Ushers: These hardworking helpers take tickets and keep an eye on the audience. So no mischief, please!

Stage Manager and Deputy Stage Manager (Clipboard Charlie): These leaders help everyone work together as a team backstage.

Actors (the Person Who Gives Her Carrots): It's not all applause for actors – they must work very hard to learn their lines. Bravo!

Animal Handlers (Big Ed): If there are animals in a show, animal handlers look after them and clean up any mess!

Green Room (the Place Where People Chat): The Green Room is not always green – it's where actors relax between performances or chat after the show.

Wardrobe (the Stupendous Space of Delicious Dresses): Here costumes are looked after and stored for the show – sometimes the team have to make quick repairs during the performance.

Wigs, Hair and Make-Up (the Room of Fluffy Stuff and Powder Puffs): From wacky wigs to fake blood, the wigs, hair and make-up team have lots of tricks up their sleeves!

Armoury (where the Pointy Pokey Things are stored): Here things like swords or spears are safely kept. Actors must learn to use the weapons correctly, so no one gets hurt.

Rehearsal Rooms (the Place People Prance; the Spot of Silly Sounds; the Hall with Pointy Pokey Things): Actors, dancers or musicians practise in rehearsal rooms – some of Lola's favourite places!

Flash and Bang Box (well … Flash and Bang Box): Here the light and sound effects are created – which is why Lola likes it!

Prop Room (the Cupboard of Tasty Treats): Props come in all shapes and sizes, from big grandfather clocks and pianos to small teacups and pens. During a show the small items are kept on the prop table next to the stage – unless Lola's around making mischief!

Set Department (the Room of Weird and Wonderful Worlds): The designer makes a small model of what they'd like the set to look like. The carpenters, metal workers and scenic artists then build and paint the real set using the small model to help them.